How I See Life

Life

VOL. 2

How I See Life
Life

VOL. 2

DAVID WRIGHT

DIPS Publishing

How I See Life, Volume 2

Published by DIP'S Publishing
Cleveland, OH

www.thinkforyourself.life

ISBN: 978-1-946818-02-7
Printed in the United States of America

This book is dedicated to my Uncle Marshall. It's dedicated to you because you are my rock. You are my family, but you treat me as an equal. You saw my mind and attributes as a child for what they were. You never made me prove my talents, you just always accepted me for what I was at the time. While always telling me all that I could become in the future. You spoke fortune into my life by caring about me. You taught me manhood, and that things aren't always easy. I learned from watching you, that a Black Man is worthy. And that we don't have to be someone else in order to succeed. I learned from watching you that being myself is always being enough. I learned from you how powerful a man's Will is in determining his future and fate. I learned that to be perfect we just need to be true and to give our all. I call my son Mr. Smith out of respect to you. Yes you are my Uncle, but you are also a man's man. Thank you for teaching me to be Man! And I don't thank you just for me, because of you I can now make my sons into men. So I thank you now for us all.

CONTENTS

How I See Life

Life

VOL. 2

In denial

My mistakes could not have been what led me here. I made poor decisions yes but I never meant things to turn out like this. I have lied, cheated, stole, and killed. But my worst enemy, a dog for that matter doesn't deserve the treatment I now receive. I have done terrible things but I still deserve pity. My choices were not the best and I have harmed many. I lost my ability to feel shame when I persisted in hurting others, but I didn't put in motion this kind of misery; I mean I take it all back now, I scream at the top of my lungs I don't deserve this. Someone please save a good man at heart; well at least in theory, I just wasn't given the opportunities to do right. My parents taught much, me not listening wasn't my fault; I was just busy with life. As I got older, they spoke more of the truth. But again I was too busy living my own life, accomplishing the impossible. If I would have listened to my mom and dad yes, I would have a stable life. But there is no excitement in stability, I could take their money but not advice. I have lost friendships but it wasn't my fault, they all stop having time. None were real because real doesn't change. Real remains the same. Real is being able to sleep on your couch. Even though your married with children of your own. Crazy the world is; I have done nothing to provoke life's wrath!

I'm weary

So tired I am of having to understand, but work on me still must be done. That is not easy to admit, but I'm done hiding from the truth. I will be honest about my short comings, to myself before anyone else. I have hid behind good deeds in the past, to cover up how very unemotional I am. I can appear cold, appear because I am. I have been through so much; that at times, I'm truly disconnected. I don't want to be apart. In bonding with the spirit I have become able to feel again. I am so very tired of me, let this entity morph into another that is eloquent; that is able! That can feel and articulate, colors, sounds and emotions. I just want to be better. Less flesh and more spirit, I am so tired of the battle! Who will win isn't my fear or concern. Just the reality I'm in, and I'm tired of the struggle. Never to give up, I only express that I'm weary.

Once

I was a boy, I thought that way and there was no harm in it. As years passed I grew in thought to see that Once I chose to be, I was. And that was anything. Once I thought I wanted to be the toughest person I knew. As time passed that became unimportant. Once it did, I desired riches to make me into the man I should be representing. Once I understood money could only change your status but brings out the real you; I again changed goals. Once I believed this the truth, I started to pursue myself. The second I did; I began to see, that once your soul is your concern, you elevate! I saw that once you care for the other you inside; it begins to show concern and care for you—the outside as well. Once we understand what is lying dormant, what is waiting to be discovered; we are alive! Once we can accept the role to be played we begin to live. Once we are free enough from ourselves to see something as important other than ourselves, we feel. Once we begin to take this charge seriously, we desire—and begin our transformation! Making word flesh! Once you do see, begin your work with haste; because there are no second chances! You get this opportunity to live this life, only Once!

Life is like traffic

People only look out for themselves, not aware or caring about another's schedule. We could yield, or let others go ahead of us but we must be there on time at the expense of all else. Another may be stranded on this road of life we live. Do we pull over and offer assistance, No; Rather we scream for them to get out of the way or simply go around. Never ever stopping to help, rarely do we put ourselves in another's shoes. We don't freely let another in, or allow a car to merge. We make others work for every opportunity; and so must we—too—race! You put your blinker on and I speed up! No compassion, no courtesy and therefore; no help is given, so subsequently no help can be received. We all are road, or life raging; can we ever calm down? Is it more work to let one in, or to keep one out? We pay no attention, just rolling. Can we not care about the other driver again? I will be the first to let you merge, so that when I need to get over, you will slow down!

My education

My education came from traveling a rocky road; by choice. I was always guided to an easier path but nevertheless seemed drawn to the roughest terrain. If not difficult it isn't correct was truly an understatement, as I, bent on self-destruction, only chased grief. It wasn't until I met pain that I was able to see life for the heaven or hell I could make of it. I grew smarter and more apt with every sin committed. Blessed to have been spared from myself until I had time to figure out—me! My education is a school in itself that we all go through but not many retain the lessons taught for prosperity. So ... we ... aren't smart. Everything we go through guides us to our destiny, on a sea of thought; traveling, some of us go with the current, while others fight against it, for no reason and often times in vein. Our goal should be to become educated and better at this job of living. So that we may pass on to the next generation, what it takes!

Personality

How you act, says a lot about who you are. Your personality is that thing that precedes you, it meets others when your physical presence is but a whisper. Trust that they will remember what they've heard. As humans we do two things perfectly: judge and remember others' mistakes. Take care to treat people with as much acceptance as you can muster. Even if their attitude doesn't warrant it. You might find this first trip rough but the next time you pass by the road will be smoother. Subtleness works to your advantage, never attempt to force, only suggest that which you wish to be done. Start in reprimand with your shortcomings as to lead by example and not by mere conversation. No man is an island to himself let your personality be befitting to the inhabitants of any land you encounter. A pleasing personality is the oil that keeps the engine of the world lubricated.

Wings

You journeyed to this earth and had me, you cared for, nourished, trained and taught. You floated through life's difficulties like an angel on wings. I watched you hover over the stove many a night making dinner or in the morning preparing breakfast from nothing. You floated over the garden creating and helping to facilitate life. Your movements are ones that I pray one day to emulate. You are majesty as praisable as my father my God. My mother what a blessing to so many, a light in the dark for some who would have not made it without you. I am in those numbers. I know you are now everywhere, all may witness your wingspan, I thank you for carrying me until I was able to carry others. To show them how to fly as you showed us. Your effects will be felt throughout time, all that we touch you do also. Your essence is woven in blessings to be felt forever. Feathers of grace and the structure of a God, worthy of praise!

Rain

Is heaven crying, does she look down on all the misery and weep uncontrollably? Is she in a state of depression because of our youth, our politics? Is she hurt because no one seems to care or because we are turning our backs on love at an alarming rate? Or is it because some go hungry on a daily basis, while some discard daily what it would take to sustain them? Does she cry because our young ladies don't regard themselves as such? Looking to be royal as they dismiss their very thrones! As she does cry and awful it is when taking place, how much more does she smile? If the rain are tears, sunshine would be a smile would it not? Times when one helps another out the blue and refuses reward! The smile of the young mother making it despite the odds! The smile of the single father braiding his daughter's hair. Days and days of smiles we receive, so much so that sometimes we beg for tears! We beg for the rain! Let us not forget the good times, they far outweigh the bad! Rain it may fall but it doesn't last forever!

Up hill

Sometimes the battle it is, what we learn from the weight of this process is what you will build your life on. The fabric of your thought is sprinkled with everything that builds your character. You are who you are, the true who you are when no one is watching. What do you say to yourself when your alone, that's you!! You can always change you but you must move up hill to do so. Chances make champions and iron sharpens iron. We are only as good as that which we come up against, embrace this journey and learn. So when you make it atop this lofty hill, YOU CAN BEGIN THE PROCESS OF PULLING UP OTHERS!

Like me

You are just like me! We look the same even I at your age thought as you do now! You are so much like me; my prayer is that you will be better! I was stubborn, please don't be! I was obsessed with always being right, please don't be! I was disrespectful, please don't be! I was ashamed of myself, please don't be! For the 10 things I did right in my life, there were 50 things done wrong. You help bring legitimacy to my other 7 choices! You being one of the 3 right things I have ever done. I want you to be better than me! I want you to prosper and succeed where I failed! To further the name, we've been entrusted! I see myself even in your thoughts! You are just like me! Be better, don't fall for the traps and tricks I fell for! Be smarter than I was! You were born just like, but grow to be better than. Please don't be like me!

My Lane

My lane, where I belong. The place where all my skills are known and put to proper use. The place where I am revered, honored, respected and looked up to. I will not remain here forever but while I'm in my lane. I will learn it fully because my yesterday's have lead me to this and this is the way to my tomorrows. Unwise would I be to skip a lane, a step, a process in the equation. Better I should enjoy my now's instead of overlooking them for my tomorrows. Math done out of sequence will always produce the wrong answer. I have failed enough; I will stay in my lane until the directions tell me otherwise!

Don't push me away

Do you know how much I love you? I don't think you do, because you push to find out. You constantly push, to see, to explore and to report on. When is enough, enough? We all use, but it's the misuse that goes noticed, that leaves a bad taste. If you ever find yourself questioning you, your pushing. If you find yourself alone when you shouldn't be you've maybe pushed too far. May I live to let my love grow? Or must the grass constantly be cut until it refuses to come through the soil? Don't push me away, I don't want to go. But I will do what I'm told. And action...speaks louder...than word.

Extended

Closer to me than any family I have ever had, our blood not matching gives rise to a new type! Extended, not from me or through me but are a part of me just the same! My brother from another's loins, you mean as much to me as if we would have come out of creation at the same time! Your actions speak louder than a warning siren when you extend to me the hand of friendship in such a way that it is perceived like the powerful fist of a brother behind, in front and on each side of me ready to do battle and back me! As I would do the same for you so have we transformed our acquaintance into something much more concrete! Something able to stand the test of time and remain unscaved! Friend is disrespectful to the bond, extended Family places you at the top, for your work determines your worth!

Who knows

What tomorrow may bring or exactly what the future will hold
All we can do is our best and have faith in the rest as we do not
exist on our own
No man is an island but how does one trust
Living blind because no manuals in print
Some things we do correct others no so much so all we can do is
look within and repent
How will we end up I guess learn as you go and attempt to
commit less mistakes
No one knows what is coming
But what I do know is this to succeed I'll do whatever it takes.

Life

I fancy the man who has life figured out as
for myself it's a hit and miss
I proceed to take a step then stumble two steps back as I've
learned many live like this
To plan courageous and execute fearless
Is what the educated man will do
If you don't seek understanding you will sit back and complain
about how life is happening to you
I want to cause an effect not be effected by cause
Like a bearer of burden for man
I want to live life fully before I'm faced with the truth that soon
it will come to an end
My life is my own and if I don't take control it can't be blamed
on anyone else
I don't grab the reins the only fool is me and for my life I will be
blaming myself.

Round and round

Round and round I go, wanting to stop but never doing so. Every time I indulge I hate myself. Every time is my last time, but I seem to keep quitting only to betray myself and start again! What is the dysfunction in me that I can't restrain my thoughts! I want what's best no different from any other person on earth! So why, I will ask again, I feel so inferior, so low because I can't discipline me. I'm scared all the time because I'm unpredictable, it's what will I do next that keeps me in constant fear. What part of God do I resemble? "My child, every thought you have is how you are in my image! You prove your power as you bring to yourself your fears! You partake but that is the effect, not the cause. Your situation is the flesh of the thought but not the feeling that gave it life! Find the cause and you will find the cure! Knowing is all of the battle, the power you receive from truth shall set you free... From yourself and going round and round."

Stone

Solid through and through, heavy in my position. Holding it down for centuries, I follow in the footsteps of many greats before me. I join their numbers! Truth in your heart must be manifested in life, I speak what is real and for us to learn and prosper from! No more rotten building materials, let us think mansions of pure gold and marble, diamond studded nails; all the finer things into existence. Pure thought leads to heaven, an attainable place with an unlocked door. Your paradise does not await you, for it is forever on your mind, what you ponder, what you constantly contemplate you receive; good or otherwise. Stone, how solid are you? Many dread this fact—this responsibility—only some can come. The rest will wait to hear your account of heaven. For all are not Stone!

Watching time pass

Some succeed and some don't as the hours transpire. But success is judged differently to all that look with a straight eye. It means so much to still have those you started with. As time passes so do friends some here, others gone or put away. On the shelf never to be dusted again. Time heals all wounds, not true as some wounds cut to the soul and so their healing must wait until the next lifetime. The sun has seen it all since the time of Cain and Abel until the lights go out and none can see. Moonlight reminds me of a time long ago when we were schooled and cared for, to be developed to make a contribution. That is all of our eternal jobs, to make a difference being utilized by the Grand One! Good job O good and faithful servant, speak to me and speak through me! Grey haired awaiting my journey home with a smile on my face, facing the sun! Watching time pass!

There are worse places than prison

Those that have been incarcerated before, can tell you how bad prison is. They know how you are deprived of a loved one's touch and even your basic rights. Those that have been locked up will admit how lonely it can be at night or how disappointed one is when he/she receives no mail. They can tell you about those holidays, birthdays and funerals missed. While telling you how the silence of concrete and steel can seem to pick at your very soul. Grown men/women trapped physically inside a box with limited light and ventilation. Doing a number of years for whatever offense committed. As hellish as this place sounds and is, I promise to you that there are worse places than prison. Those of us whose bodies are free but minds are trapped amongst the demons of thought, will tell you, there are worst places than prison. Men/women that have experienced heartache and relive it daily in their minds, can tell you that there are worst places than prison. When your physically free but your thoughts are hurting your life. Tell me honestly that you can't say; there are worse places than prison.

I'm still here

All that was done against me, I'm still here, a little bruised but smarter and more prepared! I was overlooked and counted out, left for dead. But when the smoked cleared, I'm still here. You can't get rid of me, every failure doesn't discourage me, it only makes me more determined! Every time I lose and don't die, I feel even stronger! I'm invincible, no fear; I'm still here. What can you do to me that hasn't already been done? I'm still here and not going anywhere!! You're going to need reinforcements if you ask me, and if what you've thrown at me is your best; you need to get a better best! Because it isn't enough, I will triumph in spite of! I am strong, I am unafraid and I am still here!

True freedom

True freedom is when you know the truth! Or at least seek it! With the fear of being fallacious, not apparent. When you don't mind being wrong in your search. In full knowledge that while you express the truth and only while your expressing it, you can never be wrong! Because the truth is omnipotent, therefore always true. Apparent genius comes from within, from that connection that can only be had from knowing the truth. We are birthed from that which sets you free from all lack, all fear and all ill-health. We are enslaved by the lies we are told. We have total control but are told we don't, we can live in heaven now but are told we must die to get there. True freedom, wealth, health and all desired is in even the very air we breathe. We must learn what is true to find freedom.

Get some rest

You did the impossible, raised a child that cares for more than himself!

Up early every morning and after hours going to sleep. For years you maintained a struggle that would have broken most!

You lived for me, my selfless teacher. Who would rather I win than you! Every hard decision made must have hurt. Strong you were not to feel but to do what's right and best. Rest well deserved, instead somehow I know your helping arranging the cosmos for the next group to achieve! Always ahead thinking and always moving to advance the cause! Rest, get some; it is well deserved!

One's maturity

What makes us mature, one man asked the next.
"Is it the pieces of grey on our head?"
Or is it the mark in the road that an older man knows at this
point something profound must be said?
If that is the case I've yet to meet the man with enough grey hairs
or wisdom to spout
A fraise that pays to un darken our days
with that of fear and doubt
For if you know, speak the words to do away with those things so
that we all may right now be free
If you have the answer say,
I await the response I listen for you to tell me
In retort to you statement I can only say this,
a man in his heart will know
Which way, left or right, should he hide, flee or fight when it's
time he will know which way to go
It isn't simple at first but as we live we learn
And understand that much more as days past
To mature is no test and the answer is simple it takes man all the
days that he has.

The train

Are you ready for the ride, be careful of those that follow because they might not be built for the journey! Many tag along, rougher the terrain the shorter the train line. When your rich you have cars on the track, when your poor your alone. I have come to only travel with a caboose. As where I'm headed few can follow. Or are willing too. It takes a special kind to make up your own mind. To question what's believed, to push through doubt of your own. It is not a fun ride, because alone it's made. But the peace I feel trumps the fun of together! To learn this good news, I will just talk to the father if none else are ready. And to share it I will search to find. But I'm taking the trip, care to join? All aboard!

Life's miles

Longer road the better, as most are in no rush to end this journey. Like the masses, we wish it could, would continue on forever! Again in most races we long for the end, but not this one! An extra lap or two has always been welcome, the races restart, in most cases would not at all be objected to. Life's miles aren't really taken full advantage of until we are close to the finish. Life's miles started out being a burden but now I readily pack my bags to take any trip worth taking. I've learned what a privilege it is to embark, time after time. How we can remember the terrane we've crossed, like the back of our hands! Every bump a character builder. Every pitfall a secret to success! Life's miles cannot be traded or traveled for another by another! What a privilege it is to be alive, logging life's miles!

I am humble

Able to be talked to and able to listen. I am humble, I know that the force works through me. I am a part but I am not it. I share but don't own, I am apart but not the only one. We are all One, together. Not known but still felt, I know. I am humble because your presence makes me so. The beauty in the flowers and trees, the masterpieces through us that are created. I am humble, I am confident but still know my place. I know that I come from a greater one, a source that knows all. A force that brings into play every perfectly choreographed movement imaginable. I live watching this process called life; and I am humble!

What else matters

When we argue and fight it seems to be all that's on my mind. But when I give it proper thought the situation seems so minute when compared to the size of our love! When I keep that on my mind, what else matters!

Pictures of the past

Remember when we used to stay up after being told to go to bed, and whispered until we fell off. Those were the days, when we would stare at the clock waiting for Christmas to come and always fell asleep before it did, strange it is I remember so vividly these things. Just like they happened yesterday. I see us laughing, riding bikes, hoping that when we went in to get a drink, we weren't forced to stay. Sitting on the garage talking, waiting for the next thing to occupy our attention. My past is like an art gallery, full of priceless master pieces. Some will make you laugh, others will make you cry, while some will leave you scratching your head. We took full advantage of a time when life wasn't so complicated with responsibilities. A time when we controlled our own lives until it was time to go inside.

Picasso couldn't have done a better job, Mona Lisa pales in comparison!

Class is out

We did what they expect us to do but we learned from our mistakes and became better at it. It takes a special mind to understand addiction to keep your finger on the pulse of impulsiveness! To understand that which is insane, loveless but lucrative as a collection plate. School was all day and all night, some graduated. Others died in class giving an answer at the black board. These were not the typical detentions! The teachers wore badges and guns and the principal kept a hammer. Sometimes it was about learning but mostly my mistakes cost. Committing mistakes as a youth carried over into adulthood now a slap on the wrist is 188 months and a second chance means come back when you get out! That I was never taught compounds my stupidity as I follow my nature in search of the best but armed with little experience, so I arm myself! And unbeknownst to me the journey begins of a life of learning based on poor choices, why did I stop learning when I thought I knew. I promise not to make that error again. Class is out but it's clear to me now that we never stop learning.

Laugh or cry

I don't mean to be morbid but when I die
I have planned so much ahead
My children won't know whether to laugh or cry while putting
the last dirt on my head
I have used my time accumulating things, furthermore it has
been well spent
On filling my kids with the words of the Lord on
how to forgive and repent
I have saved much for them houses and things,
Roth IRAs for sure
But the love they've learned and respect they have for themselves
I know will be valued much more.
Possessions they fade as things often do.
But what I've left
I'm sure when I die
My kids will sit around, stare and look at each other not
knowing whether to laugh or cry.

Reactions

I think about the things I think about some
bring joy and others grief
The things I think about are held inside due to belief
Never released therefore I am constantly in a spell
Of reactions based on actions and I don't know from whence
they hail
My father spoke of things I followed him
due to my respect
I hold dear the things he thought and taught but now I must
think for myself
I make mistakes but I can trace the action right back to its start
Now my reactions are based on actuals and not just emotions of
the heart
Because I cry and feel deep inside is no reason not
to question truth
I factually base my reactions so I know what I'm reacting to.

The marathon

On your marks, get set, GO. This race is for your life. It is not a sprint however; it is a marathon! Therefore, pace is epic. One must develop a rhythm to be able to hang in there. Runners that lose ground are trampled, so slowing isn't an option! We are winners, as we expect greatness from ourselves so do those in training. As imitation is the best form of flattery be careful, you never know who is watching you run, such an impact we have on young onlookers who know not, just yet how to keep up. Role models, coaches, trainers are we all because our aptitude for long wind running wasn't gained alone or overnight. We developed, we were developed as we still grow learning new things no matter how long we've been running. This marathon is for me to learn myself, as I go, I find out more than I ever knew. I encourage, I am encouraged. I train to be the best, I freely show others the way. On your marks get set, let's go. See you at the finish line! Make sure you don't finish alone!

Let's get it

It is time to never fear again, let's get it. It is time for us to unite and stand together to achieve every hope, dream and wish we can come up with. It is time to break off the chains and shackles of competition that enslave us all. Now is the time, let's get it. Only together will we be strong enough, together in spirit and mind. For where a man's thoughts are, his body will follow. We must rise up against untruth no matter how uncomfortable it makes us. It is time to stop cutting our noses to spite our face. In his image we are all one, that must be our focus! For If we are one here then we are one everywhere and the world has finally shrunk to a more understandable and maintainable size! Not a one world government but a one world brotherhood a one world civilization. Where all live and lead by virtue of themselves and no one is ruler! If the few lead the many suffer. If we all lead we all share in any suffering, which naturally will make it lighter. It's time. Let's Get It!

Broken thoughts

Like glass I have you shined from top to bottom, the perfect scenario. In my mind I see just the reflection of how I see things being. Then like a rock, or a baseball hit from the alley by kids playing. Here comes this baseball, this negative thought. Not hurled at my window by another NO. It is me who sits in front of by house and hails bricks, baseballs, rocks and any other type of unsuccessful thoughts I let linger in my head. These thoughts, these rocks are damaging my vision. So as it comes to fruition, I know not how I summoned this junk. This beat up thing of beauty I once saw. This thing resembled a gift fit for royalty but now it looks like a broken window. My broken thoughts have destroyed what I saw. Had I stayed confident maybe it would more closely resemble what I in mind constructed. Had I not doubted, I bet I would be marveling at my creation. Instead of now thinking up ways to rid myself of this new lump. I think blessings but contemplate curse, I need to change how I PERCEIVE things. I need to fix my BROKEN THOUGHTS!

Stars

When I look up I feel that my family is looking at me the same as I am looking at them.

What if we're not alone only connected from the hip to those millions of miles away? Are my thoughts mine or are they recycled over eons of time, reaching me at the very moment I need. I wonder is my future in the past as thoughts travel on vibrations as light does and we receive that in the past. I wonder when I look up am I really looking at my future my end or my beginning. The stars, what secrets do they hold ready to be discovered by one that is interested? Are we prepared for the answers or too comfortable in this blissful ignorance?

The stars, they shine like diamonds and I'm sure possess far greater riches than that.

We have been told they do.

For now, all I am sure of is that they twinkle.

Suicide

LIFE: It does get rough; I can't begin to imagine your pain, can you tell me? If nothing else but to help others and shed light on this darkness of feeling alone?!

My story of hopelessness is a brief one. I cried out for help, but as I didn't know how to, my voice may have gone unheard. My mother thought I was being moody, how could I tell her; as strong as she is, that I was contemplating giving up. My dad was always so busy providing, that I didn't want to bother him. When I tried to talk, he was often so tired that I just couldn't annoy him with me. I know you both will miss my presence but maybe it's better of this way. As I feel like I'm in the way. In a full house, I'm totally alone. In the morning we all go our separate ways, we never talk. I need to share, if I would have from the beginning these problems now wouldn't be so heavy. As it stands, I can barely breathe under their weight. My chest is so tight all the time, I live in a cage with legs.

My teachers have so many to deal with, and honestly I feel embarrassed to tell them. Please notice when one around you has a trapped look on their face. Step outside of you own busyness and ask. Don't wait, because I couldn't wait anymore. I needed help, I know you cared and loved me, and I truly forgive your lack of energy (as I know you had to work and we're tired), your lack of patience (because you were stressed out from your own life) and your lack of understanding (because I know you didn't). Have time, make time, because those around you, right under your nose—just may need your help!!

Listen to this

You're inferior, not good enough, only fit to shine my shoes
You're so dumb, well hide the facts and then misrepresent the clues
Give all of them the tools but they'll be broken and won't work
Then when the job doesn't get completed
Well make them work for half their worth
When one makes it up well sink him,
What if the people love him so
These lies will be so well-crafted even his own
mother wouldn't know.
What if the people ban together?
there's no unity so there's no chance,
Maybe once upon a time in a different life and circumstance.
We had formidable opponents now they've been crippled everyone
Not physically you see we Google attack they're young
Feed them synthetic foods and drugs enough to fill the seven seas
Give what it takes to make you sick then charge for treatment of
the disease
Make them chase their tales that's a race that can't be won
Brutally murder their leaders to terrorize the ones
That would carry on the struggle and tell the people raise their fist
Now what would you be like if all your life you were told listen
to this.

Have you seen me

I have been looking for quite some time
Because the me that I am when I close my eyes is not the one
that I want to find
In front of the mirror when I open them up
For we both know the secrets kept
From the rest of the world in this façade and image under the
mask that we call yourself
I am perfect, not really
but that's what I would have you think
In my mind and my thoughts and every fiber of my being I focus
on lack so I continue to sink
Deeper and deeper lower and lower down down down
Like a spiral staircase that leads to no place
Less to the loss but not found
Mental image is held of what it once was like
Being carefree and knowing myself
But under the strains of life, bills and the like I haven't any time
for much else
Like my wife, my children my own mental health and that's just
to name a few
while in danger of losing myself in this mess
I'm in danger of losing each of you!

Family

Yesterday you could count on, today not so much.
Through the years and tears laughter and fears we've seen to have
fell out of touch.
Now one can do that wrong and no longer family will he be
The dreaded forest lumber jack is killing of our family tree.
Connected not are we, Sunday dinner is no more
Getting everyone to come to a funeral has now become the
chore.
We only gather for the dead, we don't assemble when your alive
Unless it's a party for you getting out of prison for the freaking
umpteenth time.
I miss the family times, the reunions where we'd catch up.
But us younger generations see no need to follow up.
Toast be made to family, like the buffalo your gone
Unless you still believe in family, I hope and pray what's read is
wrong.

Cancer

Where did you come from, you are so hateful! No remorse do you have or show! Remission is a beautiful thing for those blessed with it but for those not so lucky you are pure hell. As you strip every piece of me away except my spirit, only because you save it for last! It makes no sense to run from you, your relentless pursuit is draining! I didn't want to give up or give in but the pain made me tired. Just too tired to continue. Please forgive me for not being strong enough, but I knew only heaven could heal me. And healing I needed. Escape, a portal to another time, space or body. Anywhere but here, too much you are cancer but you will meet your match one day. I hope and pray if only for your next victim's sake!

Say more

Next time I will say more. I thought that I said enough, but obviously I didn't because today you aren't here. We had a good talk our last time together. I believed what was said could carry you over until we met again. But no. I come now to share your company and your nowhere in sight. I wish I could have done something different. I will say more if I ever get that chance again. You were worth me giving my best and even tho I thought I did. Next time, with another soul, I will go above and beyond in my efforts. So there will be no discrepancies as to my performance. I would give anything at this point in my life to have the chance in yours, to SAY MORE.

As I walked away

I saw your smiling face as I walked away, knowing full well this day was coming. I never really prepared for it though. As times flies when you're having fun, I really just didn't get the chance to. You are such a pleasure to me, what you have become is phenomenal! I will never take the credit for you, only proclaim to all that will hear, that I am honored to have been apart. As I know the journey is just beginning, it will never be the same as it started again. You cannot go backwards so some things will never be. All the better because we have experienced you this way, it is time for the next chapter in your life. I bow to you becoming great because I know what you have in store for the world! I know what kind of man love, fire and pressure has created. I felt honored, I felt proud, I felt blessed when I dropped you of at college, as I walked away!

When I was big

I've been here before, my soul is old and familiar with these surroundings. When I was big, I had it all. Now I must start over in this body. My spirit has settled here, I gather my thoughts and begin again. I know my way, when I was big I traveled these same roads. I draw on the knowledge of my past to navigate my way. There is an infinite pool of wisdom I draw from. When I was big! No matter is ever destroyed only regurgitated into new form. As the old form dissipates a new one is created. The same but new. Become one with yourself and be introduced to all you have experienced over the eons! You know everything if you would only ask. This form can achieve much when guided by the past into the future. When listened to and heeded when direction is given. Your little voice inside you knows the way because this is its umpteenth time around the track. Peace be still refers to listening to your past self, when you were big.

That leaf

Over the years we have been through many ups and downs, through it all your friendship was consistent and as long as I knew where to go I always had the best of you. My friend that doesn't speak, the friend that only listens and understands. Never have you attempted to introduce me to someone stronger that you. As a youth I had no knowledge of your true personality. But I learned. Our mellow relationship has always been enough for the both of us. True I have cheated before but I always come home. As I haven't left you for some 20 years now I would believe I'm here to stay. Big or small quantity you mean so much to one who has none of you. You have gotten me through many sad and joyous occasions alike. In my deepest thoughts you are there forever pushing me to dive deeper in to find out more. Your understanding has never been matched by any other. You don't require my love, only my friendship as we have parted ways in the past with no hard feelings. Only to have hooked back up sometime down the road. That leaf, I have never had a friend that I didn't mind spending money on like I do you. Your nonjudgmental attitude is why we have been friends for so long. I can't wait until April 20 to celebrate another year. See you soon!

Anonymously

I give my secrets anonymously, trust in their authenticity! Save your money and take as many chances as you can while your young. Invest, put money into making money, remember, millionaires have 6 incomes and billionaires 13. Disregard spending, there will be plenty of time for that, better to be wealthy than to look rich. Hustle as hard as you can and save, good times won't last always. Prepare for the hard times around the corner as you know that they are on their way. Whatever your grind, on re-up day go for broke, if you lose you lose but when you win, your gamble will be worth more. Springboard into legal business. In business is God, you will learn you. In business you must trust in him, when he is know where in sight. In business there are no handouts unless it's proven you don't need one. Through monetary struggle you find God! He is in every part of business. To succeed in business, you must believe first in your product then in the market but most of all in yourself, that is the true definition of faith; belief, belief, belief. Learn the rules and spend what it takes to win. Unless you spend you won't make. Treat your business partners like family, never let anything come between you and a profitable relationship. I say this anonymously because I am the wealthy man, you thought never had a dime. And I'd prefer...

...To keep it that way!

How I feel

Sitting just thinking about a lot. The time that has passed and the people with it. Many were so good to me, I am who I am because of you, only able to feel because you taught me how to. I must have been on someone's mind when spirits were handed out. I received two share, one for me and one for the world, I am always in perfect company. I fall only to rise up stronger than I fell, I should fall on purpose more often! Out of the scars come abilities great, super human. Able to leap troublesome thoughts in a single bound. Able to share in another's problem and help, listen and contribute with no motive other than their success and their reception of light. Able I am to care for caring's sake, that I see you in need, I will give! Automatically, without hesitation for that is my core! That I give, I receive, for receptions sake. The law of retaliation, I will give love until my last breath, and receive the same!

Fly away

Inside these walls I am captured, if I could just fly away. I don't want to die here, how many times can a man answer for the same crime? I look into the sky and I feel free if just for a second. Then a step is taken and I'm brought crashing back to reality. We all have done wrong, I'm in a baseball game where my life hangs in the balance, my third strike was a pack of gum. Each stick represents a decade, as I am 50, I doubt I'll make it much further that 100. Forgive me, rewrite the laws that are meant to hide me away! I admit now let me fly away, however briefly let me know true freedom! Before I'm carried out, in my dreams let me be a bird, anything with wings. Unfair has no place in a man's vocabulary, I just don't want to die before I soar above and look down upon my choices!

Pain

Now I could tell you that I have pain figured out, but human I am and hurt I do. My mom used to say don't let anyone steal your dreams, I never knew what that meant until I felt pain for the first time. Pain can make you quit, give up, throw in the towel, she knew then what I know now. Don't pay attention to pain, you must work through it. The second you stop to complain, comment or even notice it, you have lost ground. Pain is a teacher, a cruel task master only if not regarded! Pain will show you what about you needs changing, whatever causes you pain; learn from. Regard pain as an honest friend one who will not sugar coat it, only tell it like it is. Always! Embrace that relationship because you can count on the truth that comes out of it! Eager we are to side step heart ache but that is what makes us that is what shapes us and molds us into who we are.

Let the pain you experience, guide you to you! Not turn you against others, it is natural to feel reluctant about its effects. But be honest, at the end of any pain full experience you have gained strength!

Dig deep

Never let one tell you where you should be, what you can do or what's best for you. When it looks hopeless like it's all over you couldn't possibly go another step not another thing can you take, DIG DEEP! Let the naysayers say what they will, DIG DEEP, let it never be said that you didn't try, give your best, your all, everything that you have. DIG DEEP all the way down inside where you have never been. Let your nails be filthy you have dug so far, at the end of this tunnel is light, is freedom is the true you on the other side. DIG DEEP, breakthrough and find the you that has been waiting to be found all your life! You can't take no for an answer, DIG DEEP what you need will be provided always as long as you are courageous enough to make the journey!